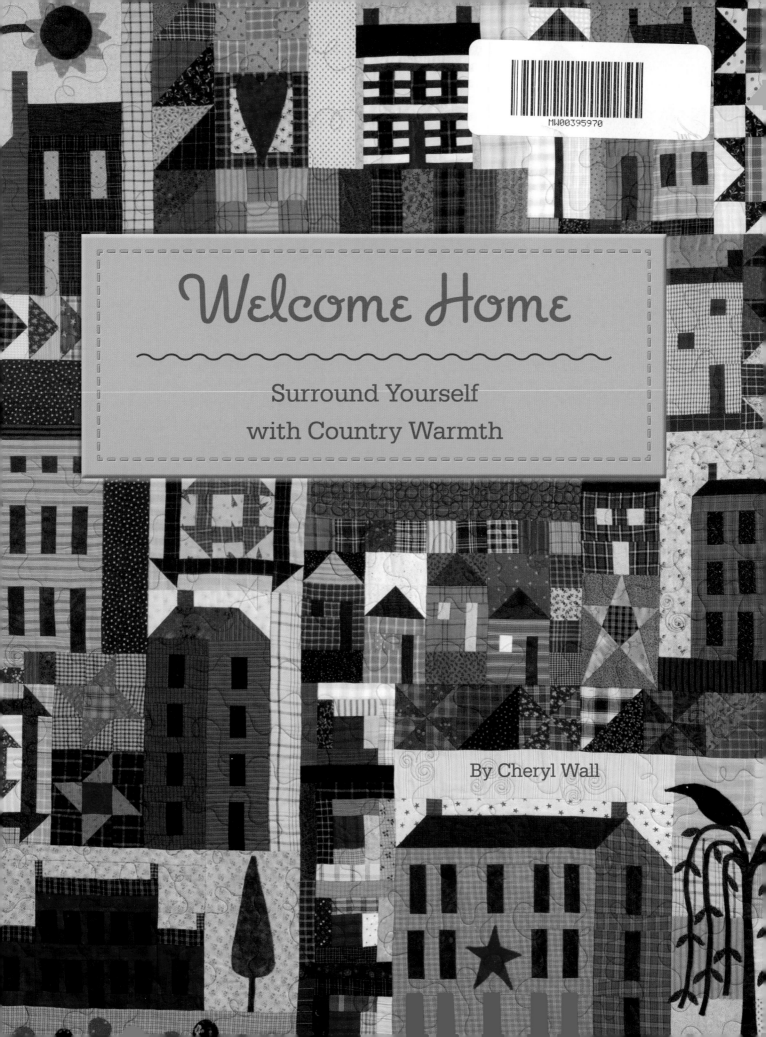

Welcome Home

Surround Yourself
with Country Warmth

By Cheryl Wall

Welcome Home

Surround Yourself with Country Warmth

By Cheryl Wall
Edited by Judy Pearlstein
Technical Edit by Kathe Dougherty
Design by Kelly Ludwig
Photographs by Aaron Leimkuehler
Illustrations by Eric Sears
Production Assistance by Jo Ann Groves

Published by Kansas City Star Books
1729 Grand Boulevard
Kansas City, Missouri 64108

First edition, first printing
ISBN: 9781611690088
Library of Congress number: 2011927826

Printed in the United States of America
By Walsworth Publishing Co.
Marceline, Missouri

To order copies, call StarInfo, 816-234-4636 (say
"Operator) KANSAS CITY STAR BOOKS

All rights reserved.
Copyright © 2011 by The Kansas City Star Co.

No part of this book may be reproduced, stored in
a retrieval system, or transmitted in any form or by
any means electronic, mechanical, photocopying,
recording or otherwise, without the prior consent of
the publisher.

PickleDish.com
The Quilter's Home Page

Dedication

This book is dedicated to my family, for instilling in me the love of home. Your pride in my accomplishments makes it all worthwhile.

Table of Contents

Mini Tutorials

About the Author

Like many addictions, it started out innocently enough. Being of a crafty bent, I decided, sometime in the mid 1980s to make a quilt. I had bought a magazine which included a pattern so simple, it could be "COMPLETED IN ONE WEEKEND!" It seemed too good to be true! I bought yards of various blue fabrics and got to work. There wasn't much actual "quilting" involved—just sewing very large squares together—and so it did go very quickly. I had made my first quilt. Ugly as sin, but there it was.

Weeks went by and I felt the urge to try another. A little more challenging this time—I decided to try making a "lap quilt" where you piece and quilt the blocks first, and sew them together afterward. I bought some rose and baby blue fabric. I used templates and handquilted everything. And proudly displayed the finished quilt on my bed for all to see and admire.

The weeks between urges to quilt were getting less and the urges were becoming stronger. I began to wonder if I was heading down some slippery slope but I was having so much fun that I didn't question myself too much. When the urge hit, I'd find a fabric shop, just waiting to sell me something. And every time I went, it seemed, there were more beautiful fabrics in colors and prints than I could ever have imagined. Patterns, magazines, and books were popping up every where. And wonder of wonders, there was this amazing new invention called the rotary cutter, which made the whole process so much quicker and easier.

Soon, I wouldn't even be finished with one quilt and the urge would hit to start another. As soon as I had a bit of cash, I'd buy more fabric. My stash was growing. My self-control was all but gone. The more I quilted, the more I wanted to quilt. I experienced something akin to panic when I found myself without a needle in my hand. I began to plan vacations around quilt shops and quilt shows I wanted to visit. I made new friends—quilting friends. I converted the basement into my quilting studio. I quit my office job so I could make quilts all day. Needing to support my habit, it was just a matter of time before I started designing my own patterns and began selling them through my website. In 2003, my business, "Country Quilts" was born.

Now, several years and many patterns and quilts later, my addiction has only grown. My days are spent stitching and my nights are spent dreaming of stitching.

My name is Cheryl.
And I am a quilt-aholic.

You are welcome to join me on my journey!
www.countryquilts.ca
www.cheryl-countryquilts.blogspot.com

Introduction

The title of this book, *Welcome Home*, was inspired by two things: house motifs, which I often use in my designs, and perhaps more importantly, the pleasure I feel when being welcomed into someone's home. I especially love homes that reflect the personalities of those who live there. Perhaps the paint is chipped in places, children's drawings are proudly displayed on the walls, the furniture bears the scars of having been passed down through generations. I love being in homes which convey a sense of warmth and welcome.

The *Welcome Home Sampler Quilt*, the main project in this book, depicts many homes, some small and humble, others larger and more stately. I've designed them in a folk-art style, each with a unique personality. I tend to get bored making quilts which repeat the same blocks over and over so I've included several different pieced blocks and some appliqué for interest. Like many of my designs, this is also a very scrappy quilt, made up of my favorite dark, rich, warm colors. But if this isn't your particular style, don't worry about matching the look. Use what you have on hand and it will reflect who you are.

"Welcome Home" is made up of several blocks, each made individually and then stitched together to form the large quilt sampler. I've also included several smaller projects, including a wallhanging, a tablerunner, a picture, and a pillow, which include a variety of techniques including embroidery and working with wool. Some of these projects are based on designs found within the main quilt and all of them were inspired by the idea of "home".

I'm not convinced there is one "right" way to quilt. Quilters tend to have favorite methods for making their projects. I've included suggestions for how to piece and appliqué your quilt but if you have a different preferred method, go for it! My personal preference is the "primitive" style of quiltmaking because I believe the imperfections in our creation reflect our humanity. Often, it's these little "mistakes" that give a quilt its charm. So don't worry if your seams don't always match or your stars have round points. Just enjoy the creative process and have fun!

It is my hope that you'll take the projects that are in this book and make them your own. And, as always, I'd love to see your versions of these designs!

Acknowledgements

So many wonderful people were a part of creating this book. My heartfelt thanks to:

- Jeanne Preto, for machine-quilting Welcome Home. As always, your gorgeous stitching finished the quilt perfectly.

- My Monday night quilting group. I don't know what I'd do without your constant friendship and support.

- The great people at Kansas City Star Publishing, for your belief in this book project and for putting it together to accurately and beautifully reflect my quilting style.

- And finally, to all of you quilters and shop owners out there, who by buying and making my patterns have allowed me to continue to feed my quilting "addiction". Thank you for being my enablers.

Welcome Home Sampler Quilt

Finished size: approximately 68" x 76"

Please read through all directions before beginning. The supply list follows on page 43 and 44.
Unless otherwise indicated, all seams are ¼" and fabrics are sewn right sides together.

Block № 1

Finished size: 24 ½" x 26 ½"

1. House Block

From house fabric, cut:

- one 1 ½" x 7 ½" strip
- one 2 ½" x 7 ½" strip

From window fabric, cut:

- one 1 ½" x 7 ½" strip

Sew together like this:

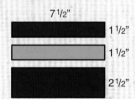

Cut crosswise every 3 ½", making 2 window strips. Discard excess.

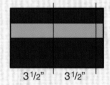

From house fabric, cut:

- one 1 ½" x 3 ½" strip

From window fabric, cut:

- one 1 ½" x 3 ½" strip

Sew together lengthwise. Sew this strip to the left of one of the window strips.

From house fabric, cut:

- one 1 ½" x 4 ½" strip. Sew this strip to the bottom of the second window strip.

From door fabric, cut:

- one 1 ½" x 4 ½" strip.

From house fabric, cut:

- one 1 ½" x 4 ½" strip.

Sew together lengthwise. Sew this strip to the left of the second window strip.

From house fabric, cut:

- one 1 ½" x 6 ½" strip
- one 2 ½" x 6 ½" strip

Sew these strips to the window strips like this:

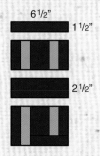

From roof fabric, cut one 2 ½" x 6 ½" strip.

From background fabric, cut one 2 ½" x 6 ½" strip.

Sew together lengthwise. Sew the roof strip to the top of the house.

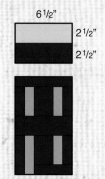

From chimney fabric, cut one 2 ½" x 10 ½" strip.

From background fabric, cut:

- one 1 ½" square

Sew the background square diagonally to one corner of the chimney strip like this:

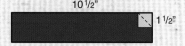

Trim the seam to ¼".

Press back.

From chimney fabric, cut one 1 ½" x 4 ½" strip.

From background fabric, cut one 1 ½" x 4 ½" strip.

Sew these strips together lengthwise. Sew this piece to the top of the chimney piece.

Sew the chimney strip to the left side of the house piece.

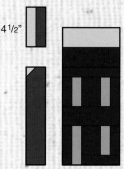

From background fabric, cut:

- one 6 ½" x 8 ½" rectangle. Sew to the top of the house piece.
- one 6 ½" x 20 ½" rectangle. Sew to the left of the house piece.
- one 2 ½" x 20 ½" rectangle. Sew to the right of the house piece.

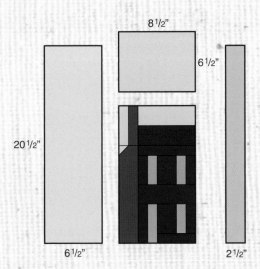

From green fabric, cut one 1 ½" x 22" bias strip. Right sides out, sew long edges together with a ¼" seam. With the seam in the back, center the stem on the background strip to the left of the house and bend over the roof. Pin and appliqué in place.

Use the freezer paper method on page 12 to cut out one flower and two leaf shapes. Pin and appliqué in place.

2. Half-Square Triangle Strip

From various contrasting fabrics cut

- ten 4 ½" squares. Put together in pairs, making five sets.

Make five half-square triangles (page 10).

Arrange the half-square triangles in a strip and sew together. Sew this strip to the right side of the house piece.

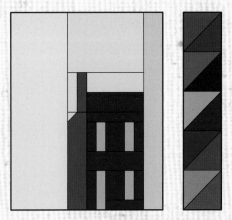

3. Flying Geese Strip

From various fabrics, cut ten 2 ½" x 4 ½" rectangles.

From each of ten various contrasting fabrics, cut two 2 ½" squares (20 total).

Make ten Flying Geese units (page 11). Sew together in a strip.

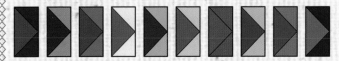

Sew this strip to the bottom of the house piece.

4. Nine Patch and Appliqued Heart Squares

For each of the two Nine-patch squares, from Fabric A cut:

- five 2 ½" squares

From Fabric B cut:

- four 2 ½" squares

Make two Nine-patch squares (See page 11).

For each of the two appliquéd heart squares, from center fabric, cut:

- one 4 ½" square

From border fabric, cut:

- two 1 ½" x 4 ½" strips. Sew to top and bottom of the center square.
- two 1 ½" x 6 ½" strips. Sew to the left and right sides of the center square.

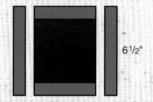

6½"

Repeat to make two of these squares. Sew to the nine-patch squares like this:

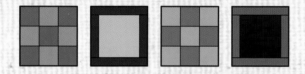

Sew this strip to the right of the house piece.

Use the heart template to cut out two hearts from red fabric. Pin and appliqué to the two squares, completing Block #1.

Mini Tutorial

Making Half-Square Triangles

Draw a diagonal line on the wrong side of the lighter square of each set.

Sew each pair together on the diagonal line.

Trim the seam to ¼".

Press back, creating the half-square triangle.

Mini Tutorial

Making Flying Geese Units

Sew one square diagonally across the end of one rectangle, like this:

2 ½"

4 ½"

Trim seam to ¼".

Press back.

Sew second matching square diagonally across the other end of the rectangle, like this:

Trim seam to ¼".

Press back, creating the Flying Geese units.

Mini Tutorial

Making Nine-Patch Blocks

Arrange squares in rows like this:

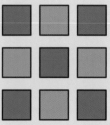

Sew the squares in each row together.

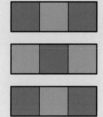

Then, sew the rows together.

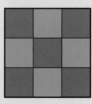

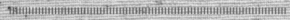

Mini Tutorial

Simple Freezer Paper Appliqué Fabric

Trace shapes onto the dull side of freezer paper and cut out roughly around the shape. Iron the freezer paper shiny side down onto the RIGHT side of the fabric. Cut out each shape about ¼" outside of the traced line. Clip curves up to the freezer paper template. Peel off the paper. You can reuse the freezer paper template several times if necessary. Don't worry if the shapes aren't identical. Pin shapes to the background and slip-stitch them in place, turning the edges under ¼" as you go.

Wool

Iron the freezer paper onto the wool and cut out on the traced line.

Block №2

Finished size: 16 ½" x 30 ½"

1. House Block

From tall house front fabric, cut:

· four 1 ½" x 9" strips

From window fabric, cut:

· three 1 ½" x 9" strips

Sew strips together lengthwise. Cut across at 1 ½", 3 ½", and 3 ½". Discard excess.

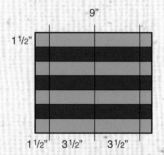

Remove and discard one window/house front piece from one of the 3 ½" window strips.

From house front fabric, cut:

· one 1 ½" x 5 ½" strip

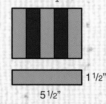

Sew this strip to the bottom of the window strip.

From door fabric, cut:

· one 1 ½" x 4 ½" strip

From house front fabric, cut:

· one 1 ½" x 4 ½" strip

Sew these strips together lengthwise. Sew this piece to the right of the window strip.

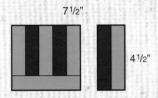

7 ½"

4 ½"

From the house front fabric, cut:

- two 2 ½" x 7 ½" strips
- one 1 ½" x 7 ½" strip

Sew these strips between the window strips like this:

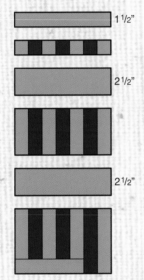

1 ½"

2 ½"

2 ½"

From roof fabric, cut:

- one 1 ½" x 7 ½" strip

From background fabric, cut:

- one 1 ½" square

Sew this background square diagonally to one end of the roof strip.

7 ½"

1 ½"

Trim seam to ¼".

Press back.

Sew the roof strip to the top of the house front.

From chimney fabric, cut:

- one 1 ½" square

From background fabric, cut:

- one 1 ½" square
- one 1 ½" x 5 ½" strip

Sew the chimney and background pieces together.

Sew this strip to the top of the roof.

5 ½" 1 ½"

1 ½"

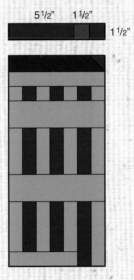

Set the tall house front piece aside.

From the small house front fabric, cut:

- two 1 ½" x 3 ½" strips

13

From window fabric, cut:

- one 1 ½" x 3 ½" strip

Sew these strips together lengthwise.

3½"

From house front fabric, cut:

- one 1 ½" x 3 ½" strip. Sew to the bottom of the window strip.
- one 2 ½" x 3 ½" strip. Sew to the top of the window strip.

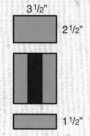

3½"

2½"

1½"

From house side fabric, cut:

- one 1 ½" x 6 ½" strip. Sew to the left side of the window strip.

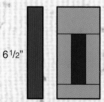

6½"

From roof fabric, cut:

- one 1 ½" x 4 ½" strip

From the house side fabric, cut: two 1 ½" squares.

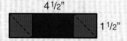

4½"

1½"

Sew squares diagonally to the roof strip.

Trim seams to ¼".

Press back.

Sew the roof piece to the top of the small house piece.

From house side fabric, cut:

- one 1 ½" x 7 ½" strip

From roof fabric, cut:

- one 1 ½" square

Sew this square diagonally to the house side strip.

1½"

7½"

Trim the seam to ¼".

Press back.

From chimney fabric, cut:

- one 1 ½" square

Sew the chimney square to the top of the house side strip.

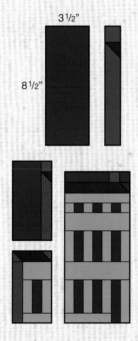

From background fabric, cut:

- one 3 ½" x 8 ½" strip

Sew this strip to the left side of the house side strip.

Sew this strip to the top of the small house piece. Sew the small house piece to the left side of the tall house piece.

From background fabric, cut:

- one 2 ½" x 15 ½" strip. Sew to the left side of the house.
- one 3 ½" x 15 ½" strip. Sew to the right side of the house.
- one 3 ½" x 16 ½" strip. Sew to the top of the house.

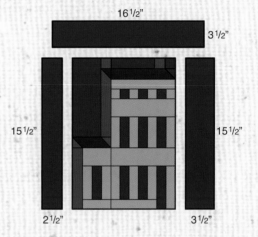

2. Friendship Stars

For each star, from background fabric, cut:

- eight 2 ½" squares

From star point fabric, cut:

- four 2 ½" squares

Sew four of the background squares diagonally to the star point squares, making four half-square triangles. *See mini-tutorial on page 10.*

From the star center fabric, cut:

- one 2 ½" square

Arrange all squares in rows like this.

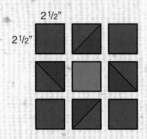

Sew squares in each row together. Then, sew rows together.

Repeat to make two Friendship Stars. Sew the stars together.

3. Double Churndash

For the small Churndash, from background fabric, cut:

- five 2 ½" squares
- four 1 ½" x 2 ½" strips

From contrasting fabric, cut:

- four 2 ½" squares
- four 1 ½" x 2 ½" strips

Sew four of the background squares diagonally to the contrasting fabric squares, making four half-square triangles. *See mini-tutorial on page 10.*

Sew the strips together lengthwise, making four pairs.

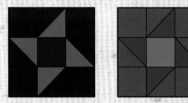

Arrange all squares in rows like this:

Sew the squares in each row together. Then, sew the rows together.

For the large Churndash, from background fabric, cut:

- four 2 ½" squares
- four 1 ½" x 6 ½" strips

From contrasting fabric, cut:

- four 2 ½" squares
- four 1 ½" x 6 ½" strips

As for the small Churndash, sew the background squares diagonally to the contrasting fabric squares.

Trim seams to ¼". Press back.

Sew the strips together lengthwise, making four pairs. Arrange the strips, half-square triangles, and the small Churndash block in rows.

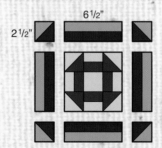

Sew pieces in each row together. Then, sew rows together.

4. Strip Filler

From various fabrics cut:

- ten 1 ½" x 2 ½" strips

Sew together lengthwise, making five pairs.

Arrange pairs in a row like this:

Sew pairs together. Sew strip filler to double Churndash.

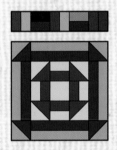

Sew this piece to the left side of the two star piece.

Sew this piece to the bottom of the house block, completing Block #2.

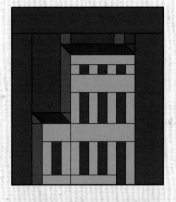

(The star in the house block will be appliquéd after the border is attached.)

Block №3

Finished size: 10 ½" x 30 ½"

1. House Block

From house front fabric, cut:

- two 2" x 12" strips

From window fabric, cut:

- one 1 ½" x 12" strip

Sew strips together lengthwise.

Cut across at 2 ½" (three times) and at 3 ½" (once).

Discard excess.

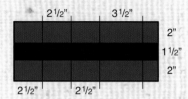

From house front fabric, cut:

- four 1 ½" x 4 ½" strips

Sew these strips between window strips.

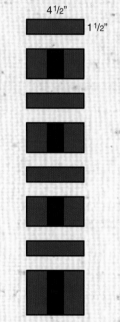

From house side fabric, cut:

- two 2" x 10 ½" strips

From window fabric, cut:

- one 1 ½" x 10 ½" strip

Sew strips together lengthwise. Cut across at 2 ½" (four times). Discard excess.

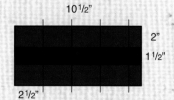

From house side fabric, cut:

- five 1 ½" x 4 ½" strips

Sew these strips between window strips.

Sew the house side to the left of the house front.

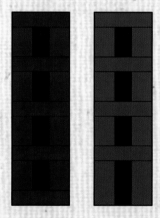

From house front fabric, cut:

- one 2 ½" x 4 ½" rectangle

From roof fabric, cut:

- one 2 ½" x 6 ½" rectangle

Sew together diagonally, like this:

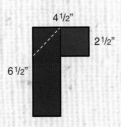

Trim seam to ¼".

Press back.

From background fabric, cut:

- two 2 ½" squares

Sew one square diagonally to the end of the roof strip.

Sew second square diagonally to the end of the house front strip.

Trim seams to ¼".

Press back.

Sew roof strip to top of house.

From chimney fabric, cut:

- one 1 ½" square

From background fabric, cut:

- one 1 ½" x 2 ½" strip
- one 1 ½" x 5 ½" strip

Sew these pieces together like this:

Sew the chimney strip to the top of the roof.

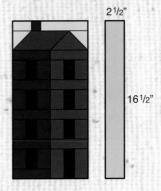

From background fabric, cut:

- one 2 ½" x 16 ½" strip

Sew to the right side of the house piece.

2. Flying Geese

Make five Flying Geese units. *See mini tutorial on page 11.*

Sew together like this:

3. Double Churndash

Make 1 Double Churndash as for Block #2.

Sew to the bottom of the Flying Geese strip.

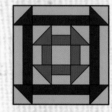

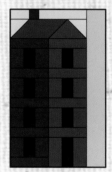

Sew this piece to the top of the House block, completing Block #3.

Block №4

Finished size: 14 ½" x 26 ½"

1. House Block

For house center, from house fabric, cut:

· three 1" x 10 ½" strips

From window fabric, cut:

· two 1 ½" x 10 ½" strips

Sew together lengthwise. Cut across every 2 ½". Discard excess.

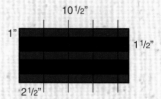

From window fabric, cut:

· one 1 ½" x 2 ½" strip

Sew this strip between two of the window strips.

From house fabric, cut:

· two 1 ½" x 4" strips

Sew these strips to the bottom of the other two window strips.

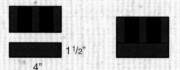

From door fabric, cut:

· one 1 ½" x 3 ½" strip

Sew this strip between the previous two window strips.

From house fabric, cut:

· two 1 ½" x 8 ½" strips

Sew one strip between the two window strips. Sew the other to the top of the unit.

From roof fabric, cut:

· one 1 ½" x 8 ½" strip

Sew this strip to the top of the house.

From chimney fabric, cut:

· two 1" x 1 ½" strips

From background fabric, cut:

· one 1 ½" x 7 ½" strip

Sew the chimney strips and the background strip together.

Sew this strip to the top of the roof.

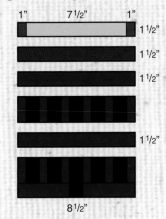

For house sides, from house fabric, cut:

· two 1 ½" x 5 ½" strips

From window fabric, cut:

· one 1 ½" x 5 ½" strip

Sew together lengthwise. Cut across at 2 ½". Discard excess.

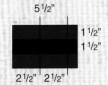

From house side fabric, cut:

· four 1 ½" x 3 ½" strips

Sew these strips to the top and bottom of the window strips.

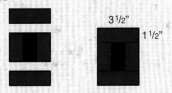

From roof fabric, cut:

· two 1 ½" x 3 ½" strips

Sew these strips to the tops of the window strips.

From chimney fabric, cut:

· two 1" x 1 ½" strips

From background fabric, cut:

· two 1 ½" x 3" strips

Sew together as shown.

Sew these strips to the tops of the house side pieces.

From background fabric, cut:

· two 3 ½" squares

Sew these squares to the tops of the house side pieces.

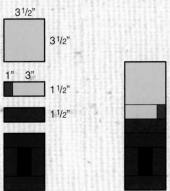

Sew the house side pieces to the right and left sides of the house center piece.

From background fabric, cut:

- one 1 ½" x 14 ½" strip. Sew to the top of the house piece.
- two 6 ½" x 10 ½" strips. Sew to the left and right sides of the house piece.

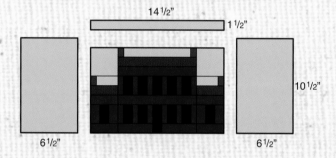

From trunk fabric, cut:

- one 1 ¼" x 6 ½" strip

With right sides out, fold in half lengthwise. Stitch with a scant ¼" seam.

Cut in half crosswise.

Measure 3" to the left and right of the house and make a crease. Center the trunks over this with the seam to the back. Pin and appliqué in place.

Use the freezer paper method *See mini tutorial on page 12.* to cut out the tree shape from green fabric. Pin and appliqué in place over trunks.

From grass fabric, cut:

- one 4 ½" x 26 ½" strip.

Sew to the bottom of the house piece.

From the flower stem fabric, cut:

- one 1 ¼" x 33" strip

Sew in half lengthwise, as you did for the tree trunks.

Cut across every 3", making eleven stems.

Pin one stem vertically on the grass strip at the house center, and two at the house sides. Pin the remaining stems at 45° angles from the center stems and the left and right edges of the grass strip. Appliqué in place.

Use the freezer paper method *(See mini tutorial on page 12.)* to cut out flower circles. Pin and appliqué in place over stems, completing Block #4.

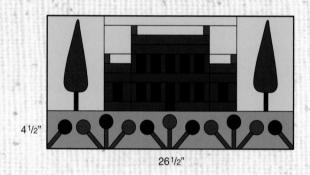

Block 5

Finished size: 16 ½" x 18 ½"

1. House Block

To make the logs for the cabin, from dark fabric, cut:

- two 1" x 12 ½" strips
- three 1" x 7 ½" strips

From light fabric, cut:

- two 1" x 12 ½" strips
- three 1" x 7 ½" strips

Sew the 12 ½" strips together lengthwise. Cut across every 1 ½", making eight strip sets. Discard excess.

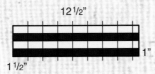

From window fabric, cut:

- five 1 ½" x 2 ½" strips (set one aside)

Sew one window between two log strips. Repeat to make four sets.

Sew the window previously set aside between two of these sets.

Sew one dark and one light 7 ½" strip together lengthwise. Repeat to make three sets.

Cut across one set at 3 ½", making two strip sets. Discard excess.

Sew these strip sets to the bottom of the two remaining window strips.

From door fabric, cut:

- one 1 ½" x 3 ½" strip

Sew the door between these two window strips.

Sew the two remaining 7 ½" strip sets, the three-window strip, and the door strip together like this:

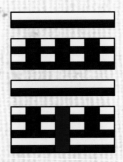

From background fabric, cut:

- two 1" x 7 ½" strips

Sew to the left and right sides of the house.

From roof fabric, cut:

- one 2 ½" x 8 ½" strip

Sew to the top of the house.

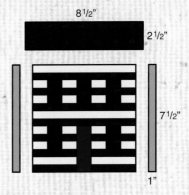

From background fabric, cut:

- two 1" x 1 ½" strips
- one 1 ½" x 5 ½" strip

From chimney fabric, cut:

- two 1 ½" squares

Sew the background strips and chimney strips together as shown.

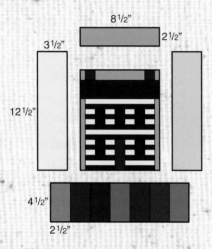

Sew this strip to the top of the house.

From background fabric, cut:

- one 2 ½" x 8 ½" strip. Sew this strip to the top of the house.
- two 3 ½" x 12 ½" strips. Sew these strips to the sides of the house.

From various fabrics cut:

- seven 2 ½" x 4 ½" strips

Sew these strips together as shown.

Sew this strip to the bottom of the house.

2. Tree

From green fabric, cut:

- three 2 ½" x 4 ½" rectangles

From each of three different background fabrics cut:

- two 2 ½" squares

Make three Flying Geese units. *See mini tutorial on page 11.* Sew together in a strip.

From brown fabric, cut:

- one 1" x 9 ½" strip

From each of two different background fabrics cut:

- one 2 ¼" x 9 ½" strip

Sew the trunk and background strips together lengthwise.

Sew the trunk strip to the bottom of the Flying Geese strip.

From various fabrics cut:

- two 1 ½" x 2 ½" strips

Sew the short ends together. Sew this strip to the bottom of the tree strip.

Sew the tree block to the right of the log cabin block, completing Block #5.

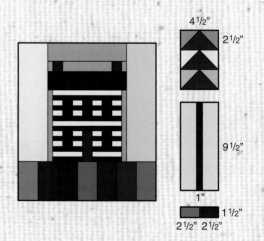

Block №6

Finished size: 16 ½" x 16 ½"

1. House Block

From house front fabric, cut:

- two 1 ½" x 9" strips

From window/door fabric, cut:

- one 1 ½" x 9" strip

Sew these strips together lengthwise. Cut across at 1 ½", 2 ½", and 4 ½". Discard excess. Set the 1 ½" strip aside.

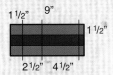

From house front fabric, cut:

- two 1 ½" x 3 ½" strips

Sew these strips between the 2 ½" and 4 ½" window/door strips.

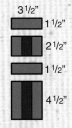

From house side fabric, cut:

- two 1" x 5 ½" strips
- one 1 ½" x 5 ½" strip

From window fabric, cut:

- two 1 ½" x 5 ½" strips

Sew these strips together lengthwise.

Cut across at every 2 ½". Discard excess.

From house side fabric, cut:

- two 1 ½" x 4 ½" strips
- one 2 ½" x 4 ½" strip

Sew these strips to the side window strips like this:

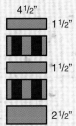

Sew the house front piece to the left of the house side piece.

From house front fabric, cut:

- one 3 ½" square

Sew this square to the 1 ½" window strip (previously set aside).

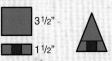

Cut out the house front template from this piece. *See mini tutorial on page 27.*

From roof fabric, cut:

- one roof template

Sew the roof piece to the right of the house front piece.

From background fabric, cut:

- one B template
- one BR template

Sew the B background piece to the left side of the house front/roof piece.

Sew the BR background piece to the right side of the house front/roof piece.

Sew this piece to the top of the house.

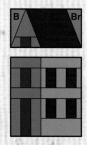

From background fabric, cut:

- two 1 ½" x 2" strips
- one 1 ½" x 3 ½" strip

From chimney fabric, cut:

- two 1" x 1 ½" strips

Sew these strips together as shown.

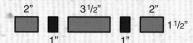

Sew to the top of the roof.

From background fabric, cut:

- one 1 ½" x 13 ½" strip. Sew to the left of the house
- one 2 ½" x 8 ½" strip. Sew to the top of the house

From various fabrics cut:

- four 1 ½" x 2 ½" strips

Sew together as shown.

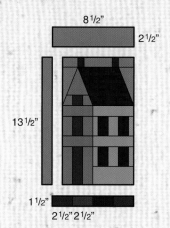

Sew this strip to the bottom of the house.

2. Sawtooth Star Blocks

For each star, from center fabric, cut:

- one 4 ½" square

From star point fabric, cut:

- eight 2 ½" squares

From background fabric, cut:

- four 2 ½" squares
- four 2 ½" x 4 ½" rectangles

Use four background rectangles and eight star point squares to make four Flying Geese units. *See mini tutorial on page 11.* Arrange pieces in rows like this:

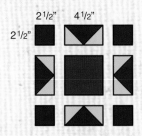 

Sew pieces in each row together.

Then, sew rows together.

Repeat to make a second star.

Sew the stars together.

Sew the star strip to the right side of the house, completing Block #6.

Mini Tutorial

Working with Templates

For me, the easiest way is to trace the template pieces onto freezer paper. Iron the pieces onto the right side of the fabric, making sure to leave ¼" all around for the seam allowance. Leave the freezer paper templates on the fabric pieces and match the points and sides of the templates. Sew the seam and remove the freezer paper.

Block Nº7

Finished size: 18 ½" x 28 ½"

1. Large House Block

From house front fabric, cut:

- two 1 ½" x 10 ½" strips
- one 1" x 10 ½" strip

From window fabric, cut:

- two 1 ½" x 10 ½" strips

Sew these strips together lengthwise like this:

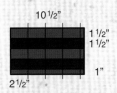

Cut across every 2 ½". Discard excess.

From window fabric, cut:

- one 1 ½" x 2 ½" strip

Sew between two of the window strips like this:

From house front fabric, cut:

- two 1 ½" x 5" strips

Sew to the bottom of the other two window strips.

From door fabric, cut:

- one 1 ½" x 3 ½" strip

Sew between these two window strips.

From house front fabric, cut:

- two 1 ½" x 10 ½" strips

Sew these strips between the window strips.

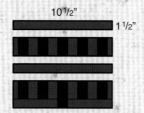

From house side fabric, cut:

- two 1" x 5 ½" strips
- one 1 ½" x 5 ½" strip

From window fabric, cut:

- two 1 ½" x 5 ½" strips

Sew these strips together lengthwise. Cut across every 2 ½". Discard excess.

From house side fabric, cut:

- three 1 ½" x 4 ½" strips

Sew these strips between the window strips.

Sew the house side to the right of the house front.

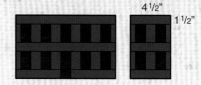

From roof fabric, cut:

- one template B
- one template C

Sew together.

See mini tutorial "Working with Templates" on page 27.

From background fabric, cut:

- one template A
- one template AR

Sew A to the left of B and sew AR to the right of C.

Sew this piece to the top of the house.

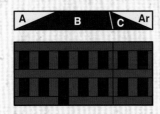

From background fabric, cut:

- two 1 ½" x 5" strips
- one 1 ½" x 3 ½" strip

From chimney fabric, cut:

- two 1 ½" squares

Sew the chimney squares and the background strips together.

Sew this strip to the top of the roof.

From star fabric, cut:

- one 1 ½" x 2 ½" strip

From striped fabric, cut:

- one 1 ½" square. Sew to the right side of the star piece.
- one 1 ½" x 3 ½" strip. Sew to the bottom of the star/striped piece.

Alternate Canadian Flag

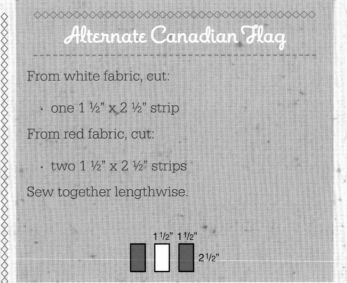

From white fabric, cut:

- one 1 ½" x 2 ½" strip

From red fabric, cut:

- two 1 ½" x 2 ½" strips

Sew together lengthwise.

From background fabric, cut:

- one 2 ½" x 11 ½" strip. Sew to the right side of the flag.
- one 2 ½" x 14 ½" strip. Sew to the bottom of the flag strip.

Sew this piece to the top of the house.

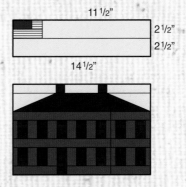

From flagpole fabric, cut:

- one 1" x 14 ½" strip

From background fabric, cut:

- one 2" x 14 ½" strip. Sew to the left of the flagpole strip. Sew this piece to the left of the house.
- one 2 ½" x 14 ½" strip. Sew to the right of the house.
- one 1 ½" x 18 ½" strip. Sew to the top of the piece.

From grass fabric, cut:

- one 3 ½" x 18 ½" strip

Sew to the bottom of the piece.

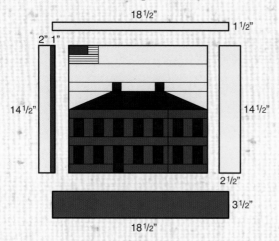

Cut out the moon shape and appliqué to the top right of the piece.

2. Small House Strip

For each of the houses, from house fabric, cut:

- one 1 ¼" x 1 ½" strip
- one 1 ½" square

From window fabric, cut:

- one 1 ¼" x 1 ½" strip

Sew the window strip between house strips.

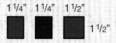

From house fabric, cut:

- one 2 ½" x 3" rectangle

Sew to the bottom of the window strip.

From door fabric, cut:

- one 1 ¼" x 3 ½" strip

From house fabric, cut:

- one 1 ¼" x 3 ½" strip.

Sew these strips together lengthwise.

Sew to the right of the window strip.

From house fabric, cut:

- one 1 ½" x 4 ½" strip

Sew to the top of the window/door piece.

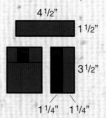

From roof fabric, cut:

- one 2 ½" x 4 ½" rectangle

From background fabric, cut:

- two 2 ½" squares

Make one Flying Geese unit *See mini tutorial on 11*.

Sew the roof to the top of the house.

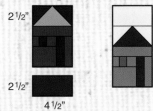

2½"

2½"

4½"

Repeat to make four houses.

From each of the four background fabrics cut:

· one 2 ½" x 4 ½" strip

Sew to the top or bottom of the houses, alternating.

Sew houses together in a strip.

From various fabrics cut:

· thirteen 2 ½" squares

Make one strip of eight squares. Sew to the top of the small house strip.

Make one strip of five squares. Sew to the right of the small house strip.

2½"

2½"

Sew this strip to the bottom of the large house piece, completing Block #7.

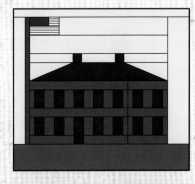

Block №8

Finished size: 16 ½" x 28 ½"

1. Large House Block

From house front fabric, cut:

· four 1 ½" x 8" strips

From window fabric, cut:

· three 1 ½" x 8" strips

Sew together lengthwise.

Cut across every 2 ½". Discard excess.

8"

1½"
1½"

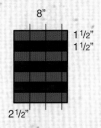

2½"

Remove one window piece from the center of one of these strips.

From house front fabric, cut:

- two 1 ½" x 3 ½" strips

Sew these strips to the bottom of the previous two window strips.

From door fabric, cut:

- one 1 ½" x 3 ½" strip

Sew between the previous two window strips.

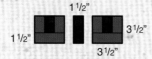

From house front fabric, cut:

- three 1 ½" x 7 ½" strips

Sew these strips between the window strips.

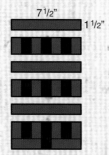

From roof fabric, cut:

- one 1 ½" x 7 ½" strip

From background fabric, cut:

- one 1 ½" square

Sew this square diagonally to one end of the roof strip.

Trim seam to ¼".

Press back.

Sew the roof strip to the top of the house front.

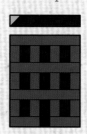

From house side fabric, cut:

- one 2 ½" x 11 ½" strip

From background fabric, cut:

- one 1 ½" square

Sew this square diagonally to one corner of the house side strip.

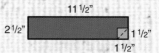

Trim seam to ¼".

Press back.

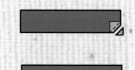

From roof fabric, cut:

- one 1 ½" square

Sew this square diagonally to the opposite corner

of the house side strip.

Trim seam to ¼".

Press back.

Sew the house side to the right side of the house front.

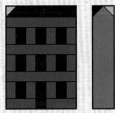

From chimney fabric, cut:

· two 1" x 1 ½" strips

From background fabric, cut:

· two 1 ½" squares
· one 1 ½" x 6 ½" strip

Sew the background fabric and chimney strips together like this:

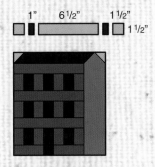

Sew this strip to the top of the house.

From background fabric, cut:

· one 2 ½" x 12 ½" strip. Sew to the left side of the house.

· one 2 ½" x 11 ½" strip. Sew to the top of the house.

From grass fabric, cut:

· one 2 ½" x 11 ½" strip. Sew to the bottom of the house.

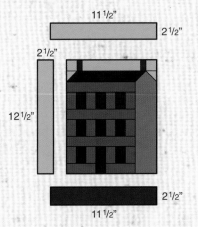

2. Stars

Make three stars. For each star:

From star point fabric, cut:

· templates A, B, D, E, F

From star center fabric, cut:

· template C

From background fabric, cut:

· templates G, H, I, J, K

See mini tutorial on "Working with Templates" on page 27.

Stitch the pieces together as directed below.

For section 1, sew piece G to the left side of piece A; sew piece H to the the right side of piece A.

Press seams toward the outer pieces.

For section 2, sew piece D to piece K. Press the seam toward piece K. Sew piece C to piece F. Press the seam toward piece C. Sew piece B to the left side of the C/F unit; sew the D/K unit to the right side of the B/C/F unit. Press the seams toward piece C.

For section 3, sew piece I to the left side of piece E. Sew piece J to the right side of piece E. Press the seams toward pieces I and J.

Sew the three sections together.

Repeat to make three stars. Set aside.

3. Small Houses

For Small House #1, from house fabric, cut:

- three 1 ½" squares
- two 2 ½" squares
- two 1 ½" x 5 ½" strips

From window/door fabric, cut:

- two 1 ½" squares
- one 1 ½" x 2 ½" strip

Arrange 1 ½" house squares and window squares in a row like this and sew together.

1 ½"   1 ½"
■ □ ■ □ ■ 1 ½"

Sew the door strip between the two 2 ½" house squares.

2 ½"
■ ▯ ■ 2 ½"
1 ½"

Arrange all strips like this and sew together.

5 ½"
1 ½"

From roof/chimney fabric, cut:

- two 1 ½" squares
- one 1 ½" x 5 ½" strip

From background fabric, cut:

- one 1 ½" x 3 ½" strip

Sew the background strip between two chimney squares.

3 ½" 1 ½"
■ ▭ ■ 1 ½"
▬▬▬ 1 ½"
5 ½"

Sew this strip to the roof strip.

Sew to the top of the house.

Arrange stars and House #1 in a strip and sew together. Set aside.

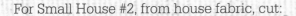

For Small House #2, from house fabric, cut:

- three 1 ½" squares
- one 1 ½" x 2 ½" strip
- one 1 ½" x 3 ½" strip
- one 2 ½" x 3 ½" strip
- one 3 ½" square
- one 3 ½" x 4 ½" strip

From window/door fabric, cut:

- two 1 ½" squares
- one 1 ½" x 3 ½" strip

Sew 1 ½" house squares to window squares like this:

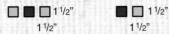

Sew the door strip to the 1 ½" x 3 ½" house strip.

Arrange pieces like this for the left and right sides of the house.

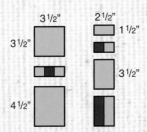

Sew the left side pieces together. Sew the right side pieces together.

Then, sew the left and right sides together.

From roof fabric, cut:

- one 1 ½" x 5 ½" strip

From chimney fabric, cut:

- one 1 ½" square

From background fabric, cut:

- one 1 ½" x 4 ½" strip. Sew to the chimney square.
- one 1 ½" x 5 ½" strip. Sew to the top of the chimney strip.

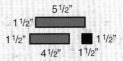

Sew this strip to the roof strip.

Sew to the top of the house.

From ground fabric, cut:

- one 1 ½" x 5 ½" strip

Sew to the bottom of the house.

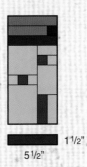

Set aside.

4. Shoofly Block

For each block, from Fabric A cut:

- five 2 ½" squares

From Fabric B cut:

- eight 2 ½" squares

Pair four Fabric A and B squares, making four half-square triangles. *See mini tutorial on page 10.*

Arrange all squares in rows like this:

Sew the squares in each row together. Then, sew rows together.

Repeat to make two Shoofly blocks. Sew the two Shoofly blocks together. Then, sew them to the right of Small House #2.

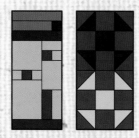

Sew this piece to the top of the Large House block. Then sew this piece to the right of the star/House #1 strip, completing Block #8.

Block №9

Finished size: 24 ½" x 34 ½"

1. House Block

From house front fabric, cut:

- two 1 ½" x 22" strips

From window fabric, cut:

- two 1 ½" x 22" strips

Sew these strips together lengthwise.

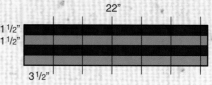

Cut across every 3 ½". Discard excess.

From house front fabric, cut:

- two 2 ½" x 3 ½" strips. Sew one strip to the right and one strip to the left of two window strips.

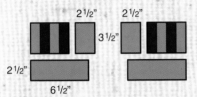

- two 2 ½" x 6 ½" strips. Sew these strips to the bottom of the two window strips.

From door fabric, cut:

- one 1 ½" x 5 ½" strip. Sew this between the two window strips.

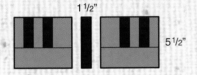

From window fabric, cut:

- one 1 ½" x 3 ½" strip

From house front fabric, cut:

- two 2 ½" x 3 ½" strips. Sew to both sides of the window strip. Sew this window piece between the top two window strips.

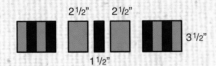

- one 3 ½" x 5 ½" strip. Sew between two middle window strips.

From house front fabric, cut:

- three 1 ½" x 13 ½" strips. Sew between all the window strips.

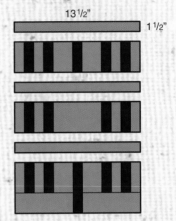

From roof fabric, cut:

- one 2 ½" x 13 ½" strip

From background fabric, cut:

- one 2 ½" square. Sew diagonally to one end of the roof strip.

Trim seam to ¼".

Press back.

Sew the roof to top of the house. Set aside.

From house side fabric, cut:

- two 2 ½" x 11" strips

From window fabric, cut:

- one 1 ½" x 11" strip

Sew together lengthwise.

Cut across every 3 ½". Discard excess.

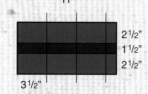

11"

2½"
1½"
2½"

3½"

From house side fabric, cut:

- two 1 ½" x 5 ½" strips. Sew between the window pieces.
- one 2 ½" x 5 ½" strip. Sew to the bottom of the window pieces.
- one 3 ½" x 5 ½" strip. Sew to the top of the window pieces.

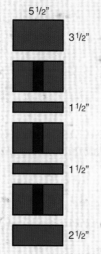

5½"

3½"

1½"

1½"

2½"

From roof fabric, cut:

- one 2 ½" square. Sew diagonally to the top left corner of the house side strip.

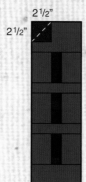

2½"

2½"

Trim seam to ¼".

Press back.

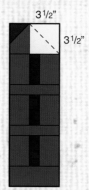

From background fabric, cut:

- one 3 ½" square. Sew diagonally to the top right corner of the house side strip.

3½"

3½"

Trim the seam to ¼".

Press back.

Sew the house side piece to the right of the house front piece, matching seams.

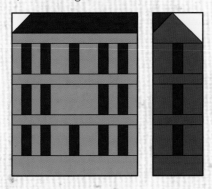

From background fabric, cut:

- one 1 ½" x 2 ½" strip
- one 1 ½" x 3 ½" strip
- one 1 ½" x 11 ½" strip

From chimney fabric, cut:

- two 1 ½" squares

Sew chimneys and background fabric together as shown.

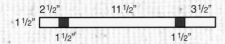

Sew this strip to the top of the roof.

From background fabric, cut:

- one 3 ½" x 18 ½" strip. Sew to the top of the house piece.

From each of eight different background fabrics cut:

- one 5 ½" square

Sew together in pairs.

Sew the pairs together in four rows.

Sew this piece to the right of the house piece.

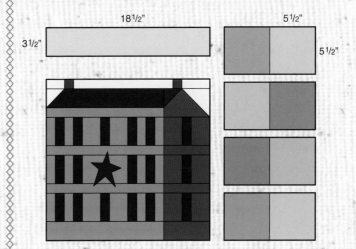

From star fabric, cut:

- one small star template

Pin and appliqué to the house above the door.

From tree fabric, cut:

- one trunk template. Pin to the center of the background piece to the right of the house.
- six bias strips, 1" x 17". *See mini tutorial on page 45.* With right sides out, sew long edges together with a 1/8" seam.

Arrange branches on background fabric, having seams at the inside edges and overlapping ends with the top of trunk. Pin in place and trim bottom ends if desired. Turn the bottom ends of branches under ¼" and appliqué the branches and trunk in place.

From black fabric, cut:

- one crow template

Pin and appliqué to the background on the top left branch of the tree. Make a French knot for his eye, using three strands of ecru embroidery floss.

From green fabric, cut:

- twenty-six leaf templates

Pin and appliqué to the branches, using the photo on page 6 as a placement guide.

2. Filler Strips

From eight different fabrics, make four 4 ½" half-square triangles (page 10).

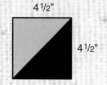

Make three Pinwheels. For each, from two different fabrics cut:

- four 2 ½" squares

Make four 2 ½" half-square triangles, for each of the three pinwheels (page 10).

Arrange these half-square triangles in rows like this:

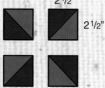

Sew pieces in each row together. Then, sew rows together.

Arrange the four half-square triangles and the

three Pinwheels in a row like this:

Sew together.

Sew to the top of the house piece.

Make four Log Cabin blocks. For each, from red fabric, cut:

- one 2 ½" square

From four different light fabrics cut:

- one 1 ½" x 2 ½" strip
- one 1 ½" x 3 ½" strip
- one 1 ½" x 4 ½" strip
- one 1 ½" x 5 ½" strip

From four different dark fabrics cut:

- one 1 ½" x 3 ½" strip
- one 1 ½" x 4 ½" strip
- one 1 ½" x 5 ½" strip
- one 1 ½" x 6 ½" strip

- Sew a 2 ½" long light strip to the top of a red square. Sew a 3 ½" light strip to the left of the square.
- Sew a 3 ½" dark strip to the bottom of the square. Sew a 4 ½" dark strip to the right of the square.

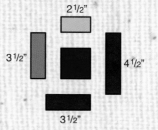

- Sew a 4 ½" long light strip to the top of the square. Sew a 5 ½" light strip to the left of the square.

- Sew a 5 ½" dark strip to the bottom of the square. Sew a 6 ½" dark strip to the right of the square.

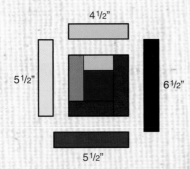

- Sew the four Log Cabin blocks together like this:

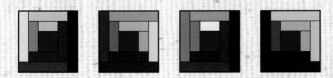

- Sew to the left of the house, completing Block #9.

Put it Together

Following the diagram on page 42:

- Sew Block #2 to the left side of Block #3.
- Sew Block #1 to the top of Block #2/3.
- Sew Block #4 to the bottom of Block #2/3, completing the left side.

- Sew Block #5 to the left side of Block #6.
- Sew Block #7 to the left side of Block #8.
- Sew Block #5/6 to the top of Block #7/8.
- Sew Block #9 to the bottom of Block #7/8, completing the right side.
- Sew left and right sides together.

From inner border fabric, cut and piece:

- two 1 ½" x 60 ½" strips. Sew to the top and bottom of the quilt top.
- two 1 ½" x 70 ½" strips. Sew to the sides of the quilt top.
- four 3 ½" squares. Use to make half-square triangles.

From outer border fabric, cut and piece:

- two 3 ½" x 62 ½" strips – Sew to the top and bottom of the quilt top.
- two 3 ½" x 70 ½" strips
- four 3 ½" squares – Pair with inner border squares to make four half-square triangles.

Sew to the ends of outer border strips. Sew strips to the sides of the quilt top.

Appliqué the star to Block #2 and the border.

Finish your quilt! *See mini tutorial on page 45.*

Block 1

Block 5

Block 6

Block 2

Block 3

Block 7

Block 8

Block 4

Block 9

Welcome Home Sampler Quilt Supplies

Tips:

Cut larger pieces from fabric first to make sure you'll have enough. Cut smaller pieces from what's left over.

Like recipes, quilters have their favorite methods for making their projects. I've included suggestions for how to piece and appliqué your quilt. If you have a different preferred method, go for it!

What You Need:

NOTE: This pattern is intended to use up a lot of scraps in your stash. However, if you haven't accumulated a large stash of scraps, measurements are included.

For the quilt:

- Freezer paper
- Pins
- Lots of scraps

Block Nº1

- Fat quarter house front fabric
- ½ yard background fabric
- Fat quarter green fabric (for stem and leaves)

Block Nº2

- Fat quarter large house front fabric
- Fat quarter background fabric
- Fat eighth window fabric

Block Nº3

- Fat quarter house front fabric
- Fat quarter house side fabric
- Fat quarter background fabric

Block Nº4

- Fat quarter house (center and side) fabric
- Fat quarter background fabric
- Fat eighth window fabric
- 5" x 27" piece of grass fabric

Block Nº5

- Fat quarter dark house fabric
- Fat quarter light house fabric
- Fat quarter background fabric
- Fat eighth window fabric

Block № 6

- Fat eighth house front fabric
- Fat eighth house side fabric
- Fat quarter background fabric

Block № 7

- Fat quarter house (front and side) fabric
- Fat quarter background fabric
- Fat eighth window fabric

Block № 8

- Fat quarter house front fabric
- Fat quarter background fabric
- Fat eighth window fabric

Block № 9

- Fat quarter house front fabric
- Fat eighth house side fabric
- Fat quarter background fabric
- Fat quarter tree fabric
- Fat quarter window fabric
- Ecru embroidery floss

Finishing

- ⅞ yard outer border fabric
- ¾ yard inner border fabric
- ½ yard binding fabric
- 4 ¼ yards backing fabric
- 76" x 84" piece of batting

Mini Tutorials

Making Bias Strips

Line up your fabric on your cutting mat so that the left edge and bottom edge are square. On your ruler, find the 45 degree marking and line it up vertically on your fabric. Move the ruler over the fabric until the measurement is the length you need. Cut along the edge of the ruler. Remove the resulting triangle on the left side and move the ruler farther right over the fabric until the measurement is the width of the strip you need. Cut along the edge of the ruler. Repeat to make as many bias strips as you need.

Fold the bias strips in half lengthwise, with the right sides out. Stitch the long edges together with a scant ¼" seam. Pin the strip to the background fabric, keeping the seam centered underneath so that it doesn't show. Slipstitch the strip in place.

Finishing Your Quilt

Cut and piece your backing fabric so that it's at least 4" larger all around than the quilt top.

Cut batting to the same size.

Layer the backing right side down, batting, and the quilt top (centered) right-side up, together. Pin or baste in place.

Quilt as desired.

Measure the sides of your quilt and add at least 12" to the measurement. Cut 2 ¼" wide strips from binding fabric and stitch together end to end to reach the desired length. Fold in half lengthwise, right sides out. Beginning near the middle of any side, align the raw edges of the binding and the quilt-top. Turn the first end over, about 1". Sew a ¼" seam to the corner, stopping ¼" from the corner. Backstitch to secure. Remove from the machine. Fold the binding strip up, and back down over itself at the corner, aligning the raw edges on the second side. Beginning where the stitching stopped on the first side, sew the binding to the second side and stop stitching ¼" from the next corner edge. Backstitch. Repeat around all four sides until you're back at the beginning of the binding. Overlap about 2", fold the last inch or so under, and sew to the end.

Trim the batting and quilt back even with the quilt top.

Turn the binding over the edge and slipstitch in place over machine stitching.

Sign and date your quilt on the back.

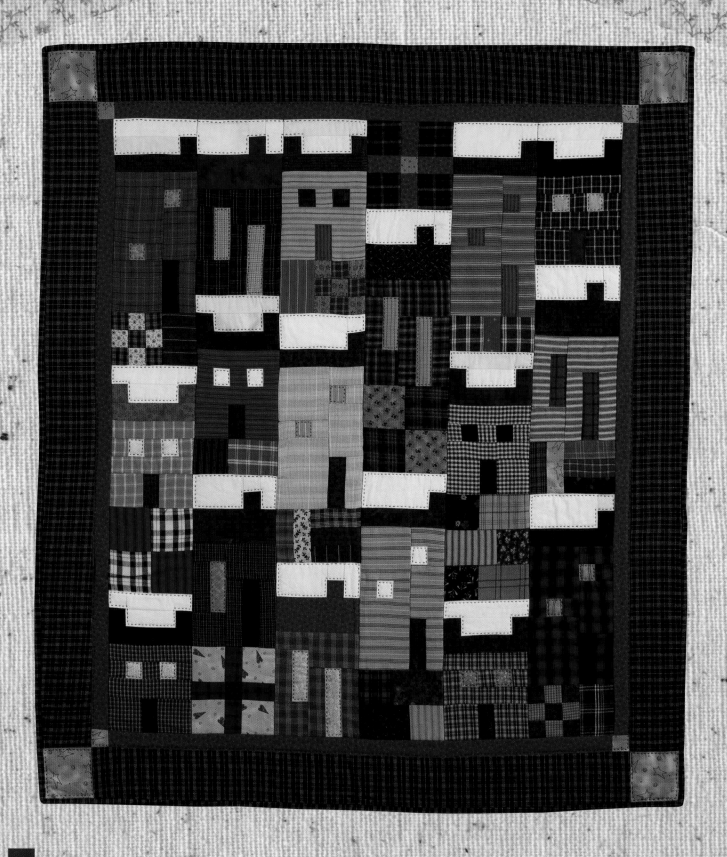

One House
Two House
Red House Blue House

Finished size: 38 ½" x 43 ½"

Please read through all instructions before beginning. The supply list follows on page 54.
Unless otherwise indicated, all seams are ¼" and fabrics are sewn right sides together.

Small House

(Make seven.)

See instructions for making small houses on page 34, under Block 8 of the Welcome Home Sampler.

For each:

- From window fabric, cut: two 1 ½" squares

- From door fabric, cut: one 1 ½" x 2 ½" strip

- From house fabric, cut:

  - three 1 ½" squares. Sew to window squares like this:

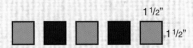

  - two 2 ½" squares. Sew to door strip like this:

  - two 1 ½" x 5 ½" strips

- Arrange all strips like this and sew together.

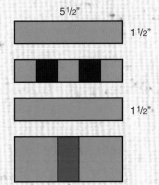

- From roof/chimney fabric, cut:
  - two 1 ½" squares
  - one 1 ½" x 5 ½" strip

- From muslin cut:
  - one 1 ½" x 3 ½" strip. Sew between the two 1 ½" chimney squares.

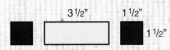

  - one 1 ½" x 5 ½" strip. Sew to the top of the chimney strip.

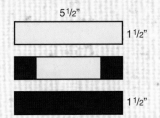

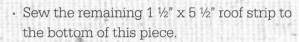

- Sew the remaining 1 ½" x 5 ½" roof strip to the bottom of this piece.

- Sew the roof piece to the top of the house piece.

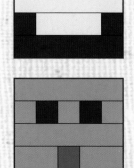

- Repeat to make seven small houses.

Medium House

(Make five.)

For each:

- From window fabric, cut: one 1 ½" x 3 ½" strip.

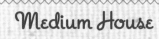

3½"
1½"

- From door fabric, cut: one 1 ½" x 4 ½" strip.

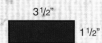

4½"
1½"

- From house fabric, cut:

  - one 1 ½" x 3 ½" strip. Sew to the window strip like this:

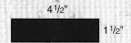

1½"
3½"

- two 1 ½" x 4 ½" strips. Sew to the door strip like this:

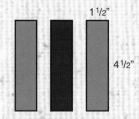

1½"
4½"

  - one 1 ½" x 2 ½" strip. Sew to the top of the window strip.

  - one 2 ½" square. Sew to the bottom of the window strip.

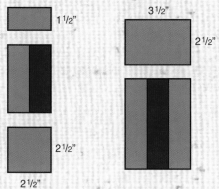

1½"
3½"
2½"
2½"
2½"

  - one 2 ½" x 3 ½" rectangle. Sew to the top of the the door strip.

- Sew window and door pieces together.

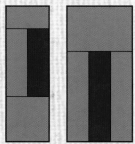

- From roof/chimney fabric, cut:

  - one 1 ½" square

  - one 2 ½" x 5 ½" rectangle

- From muslin cut:
  - one 1 ½" square. Sew to the 1 ½" chimney square.

  - one 1 ½" x 2 ½" strip. Sew to the right of the chimney strip.

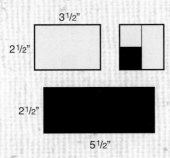

  - one 2 ½" x 3 ½" rectangle. Sew to the left of the chimney piece.

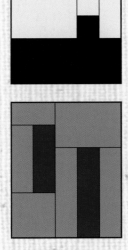

- Sew the remaining 2 ½" x 5 ½" roof rectangle to the bottom of this piece.
- Sew the roof piece to the top of the house piece.

- Repeat to make five medium houses.

Large House

(Make five.)

For instructions on making large houses see page 35 under Block 8 of the Welcome Home Sampler.

For each:

- From window fabric, cut: two 1 ½" squares
- From door fabric, cut: one 1 ½" x 3 ½" strip
- From house fabric, cut:
  - three 1 ½" squares. Sew to window squares like this:

  - one 1 ½" x 3 ½" strip. Sew to the door strip like this:

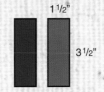

  - one 1 ½" x 2 ½" strip. Sew to the top of the 2-piece window strip.

  - one 3 ½" square. Sew to the top of the 3-piece window strip.

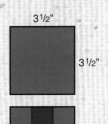

49

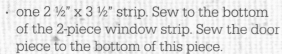

- one 2 ½" x 3 ½" strip. Sew to the bottom of the 2-piece window strip. Sew the door piece to the bottom of this piece.

2½"

3½"

- one 3 ½" x 4 ½" rectangle. Sew to the bottom of the 3-piece window strip.

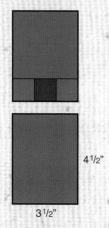

4½"

3½"

- Sew the window and door pieces together.

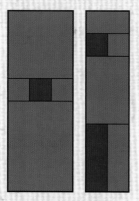

- From roof/chimney fabric, cut:
  - one 1 ½" square
  - one 1 ½" x 5 ½" rectangle
- From muslin cut:
  - one 1 ½" square. Sew to the 1 ½" chimney square.
  - one 2 ½" x 4 ½" rectangle. Sew to the left of the chimney piece.

1½" 1½"

1½"

4½"

2½"

- Sew the remaining 1 ½" x 5 ½" roof rectangle to the bottom of this piece.

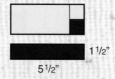

1½"

5½"

- Sew the roof piece to the top of the house piece.

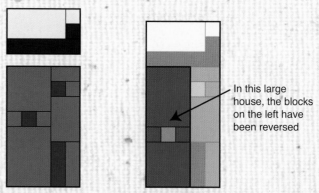

In this large house, the blocks on the left have been reversed

- Repeat to make five large houses.

For a bit of interest, change some of the blocks around within one or two of the houses. See the example above.

Filler Strips and Blocks

Nine-Patch Strips (Make three.)

For each:

- From Fabric A cut: five 1 ½" squares
- From Fabric B cut: four 1 ½" squares

See page 11 for instructions on making Nine-Patch blocks.

From another fabric, cut one 2 ½" x 3 ½" rectangle. Sew to the side of the Nine-Patch block.

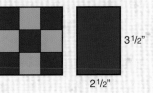

Repeat to make three Nine-Patch strips.

Four-Patch Blocks (Make two.)

For <u>each</u>:

- From Fabric A cut: two 3" squares.
- From Fabric B cut: two 3" squares.

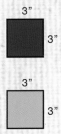

- Sew Fabric A square to Fabric B square.

- Sew strips together in rows like this:

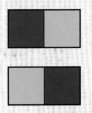

- Repeat to make two Four-Patch blocks.

Square/Rectangle Strips (Make one single, one double, one triple.)

To make a single strip, from Fabric A cut: one 2 ½" square.

From Fabric B cut: one 2 ½" x 3 ½" rectangle.

Sew together like this:

For the double strip, cut two Fabric A squares and two Fabric B rectangles. Sew together like this:

For a triple strip, cut three Fabric A squares and three Fabric B rectangles. Sew together like this:

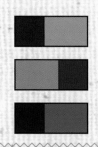

~~~~~~

Cross Blocks

(Make two whole, one half.)

For each whole cross block:

- From Fabric A cut: four 2 ½" squares.

2½"
2½"

- From Fabric B cut: four 1 ½" x 2 ½" rectangles.

1½"
2½"

- From Fabric C cut: one 1 ½" square.

1½"
1½"

Arrange pieces in rows like this:

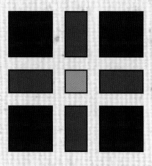

Sew pieces in each row together.

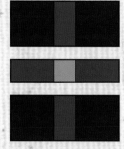

Then, sew the rows together.

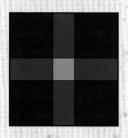

Repeat to make two whole cross blocks.

For a cross half-block, sew two Fabric A squares and one Fabric B rectangle together like this:

~~~~~~

Strip Rail Strips

(Make two.)

For each:

- From five different fabrics cut: one 1 ½" x 3 ½" rectangle from each.

Sewing together lengthwise, make one 3-strip piece and one 2-strip piece.

Sew together like this:

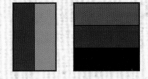

Repeat to make two Strip Rail strips.

Arrange all pieces in columns as shown below.

Sew pieces in each column together.

Then, sew columns together.

Borders

Note: Since stitching can vary, measure through the width and length through the center before cutting borders.

From border corner fabric, cut:

- four 1 ½" squares
- four 3 ½" squares

Set aside.

From inner border fabric, cut:

- two 1 ½" x 30 ½" strips. Sew to the top and the bottom of the quilt top.
- two 1 ½" x 35 ½" strips. Sew 1 ½" corner squares to the ends of these strips. Sew to the sides of the quilt top.

From outer border fabric, cut:

- two 3 ½" x 32 ½" strips. Sew to the top and bottom of the quilt top.
- two 3 ½" x 37 ½" strips. Sew 3 ½" corner squares to the ends of these strips. Sew to the sides of the quilt top.

Finish the Quilt!

See the instructions on page 45.

What You Need

- ¼ yard muslin
- ¼ yard inner border fabric
- ½ yard outer border fabric
- 2 yards backing fabric
- ½ yard binding fabric
- 46" x 51" piece of batting
- Lots of scraps

Flying Geese and Crows Wallhanging

Finished size: 39" square

Please read through all instructions before beginning. Unless otherwise, indicated, all seams are ¼" and fabrics are sewn right sides together.

House Block

From house fabric, cut two 1 ½" x 10 ½" strips.

From window fabric, cut one 1 ½" x 10 ½" strip.

Sew together lengthwise. Cut across every 2 ½".

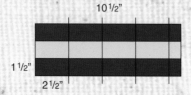

From house fabric, cut two 1 ½" x 3 ½" strips. Sew to the bottom of two window strips.

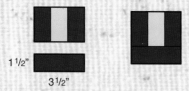

From door fabric, cut one 1 ½" x 3 ½" strip. Sew between these two window strips.

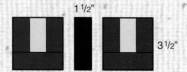

From window fabric, cut one 1 ½" x 2 ½" strip. Sew between the other two window strips.

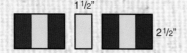

From house fabric, cut two 1 ½" x 7 ½" strips. Sew between the window strips.

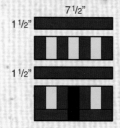

From roof fabric, cut one 1 ½" x 7 ½" strip. Sew to the top of the house piece.

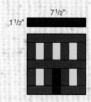

From the chimney fabric, cut two 1 ½" squares.

From background fabric, cut one 1 ½" x 5 ½" strip. Sew this strip between the two chimney squares.

Sew this strip to the top of the roof.

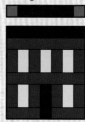

From background fabric, cut

- two 2" x 9 ½" strips. Sew to the sides of the house.

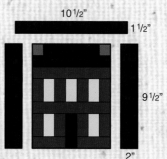

- one 1 ½" x 10 ½" strip. Sew to the top of the house. Make creases at the center of the sides and the top and bottom of the house.

- two 8" squares. Cut in half diagonally.

Discard one of the triangles. Make a crease in the center long edge of the three remaining triangles. Match this crease to the crease in the house sides. Pin and sew together. Match the crease in the remaining background triangle to the crease in the house top. Pin and sew together.

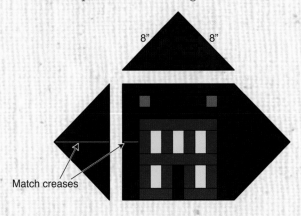

Match creases

From grass fabric, cut one 8" square. Cut in half diagonally. Discard one of the triangles. Make a crease in the center long edge of the remaining triangle. Match this crease to the crease in the house bottom. Pin and sew together.

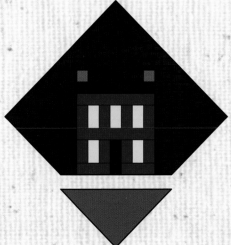

Press the house block and square it off to make the edges 14 ½" long.

Flying Geese and Four Patch Units

From each of 28 different fabrics, cut one 2 ½" x 4 ½" rectangle.

From each of 28 other fabrics, cut two 2 ½" squares.

Make 28 Flying Geese units.

See mini tutorial on page 11.

Sew into four strips of seven Flying Geese units each. Sew two of these strips to opposite sides of the house block, as shown.

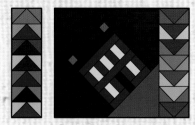

From each of two different fabrics cut two 2 ½" squares. Sew squares together in pairs. Then sew the pairs together.

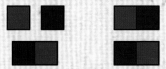

Repeat to make 4 Four-Patch units.

Sew these Four Patch units to the ends of the remaining two Flying Geese strips.

Sew these strips to the remaining two sides of the house block, as shown.

Appliquéd Corners

From background fabric, cut two 16 ½" squares. Cut in half diagonally. Make a crease in the long edges of these triangles. Match the crease in two of these triangles to the center of the opposite sides of the Flying Geese strips. Pin and sew together.

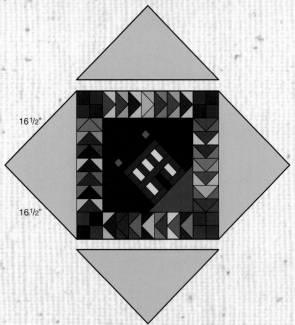

16½"

16½"

Repeat with the remaining two triangles.

Press the house block. Line up your ruler to ¼" past the points where the background triangles

meet and trim away excess fabric if necessary. The sides of the resulting square should now measure 31 ½" long.

From the vine fabric, cut four 1 ½" x 25" BIAS strips. Sew the long edges together lengthwise, right sides out. Pin in a curved shape to the corner triangles as in the photo (page 55), having the ends overlap the center of the Four-patch squares. Trim the ends to 1" and turn under.

Appliqué in place.

Using templates for Block #9 in *Welcome Home* (page 77), cut out four crow shapes and one small star. Use the template in Block #4 (page 72) to cut out 16 circles. Pin and appliqué in place, as in photo (page 55). *See mini tutorial on page 12.*

Use six strands of tan floss to make a French knot indicating the crow's eye.

Borders

From each of two different fabrics cut four 1 ½" x 31 ½" strips. Sew together lengthwise in pairs.

31½"

1½"

1½"

From a third fabric, cut four 2 ½" x 31 ½" strips.

Sew these strips lengthwise to the strip pairs, making four strip units.

31½"

2½"

Sew two of these strip units to the sides of the quilt.

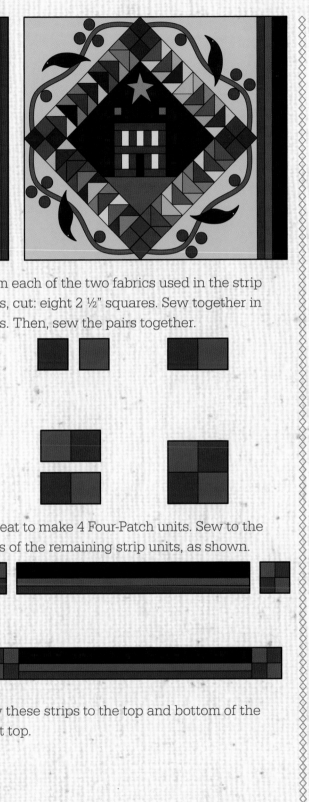

From each of the two fabrics used in the strip pairs, cut: eight 2 ½" squares. Sew together in pairs. Then, sew the pairs together.

Repeat to make 4 Four-Patch units. Sew to the ends of the remaining strip units, as shown.

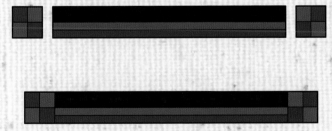

Sew these strips to the top and bottom of the quilt top.

Finish the Quilt!

See the mini tutorial on page 45.

What You Need

- ¾ yard green fabric for vine and grass
- ⅓ yard star background fabric
- ½ yard tan check background fabric
- Fat eighth red fabric for berries
- Fat eighth black fabric for crows
- ¼ yard fabric for inner border
- ¼ yard fabric for middle border
- ⅓ yard fabric for outer border
- 2 yards backing fabric
- ½ yard binding fabric
- 47" square batting
- Lots of scraps

Love at Home Pillow

Finished size: 12" square

Please read through all instructions before beginning. Unless otherwise indicated, all seams are ¼" and fabrics are sewn right sides together.

Templates are on page 78.

Use freezer paper method to cut out the following:

- From pumpkin colored wool, cut six flower petal circles.
- From brown wool:
  - six flower centers
  - one house roof
- From yellow wool, cut one house.
- From rust colored wool, cut:
  - one chimney
  - one door
- From black wool, cut eight windows. (Cut a strip ¼" x 2" and then cut across every ¼").
- From green wool, cut eight leaves.

Whipstitch the door to the house with two strands of matching embroidery floss.

Stitch the windows to the house using two strands of yellow floss to make large cross-stitches across each window.

- From black wool, cut one 9" square.
- From green wool, cut two ¼" x 13" strips.

Arrange in a heart shape on the black square. Pin and whipstitch in place with two strands of black embroidery floss.

Center the house between the stems with the bottom edge about 2 ¾" from the bottom edge of the black wool. Whipstitch the house to the black wool with two strands of yellow floss. Whipstitch the roof to the top of the house with two strands of brown floss and then whipstitch the chimney to the top of the house with two strands of matching floss.

Arrange the flower circles and centers around the stems. Make little cross-stitches with two strands of yellow floss in the flower centers to hold them in place. Leave the petals unstitched to create some depth.

Whipstitch the leaves in place with two strands of dark green floss.

Make five groups of three French knots each around stems, using six strands of yellow floss.

From green ticking fabric, cut three 12 ½" squares. Set two aside.

Center the black wool square on the right side of the ticking square and pin in place. Blanket stitch around the black wool square with two strands of dark green floss.

Press back one edge of each of the remaining ticking squares, 3 ½" to the wrong side, making two folded back pieces.

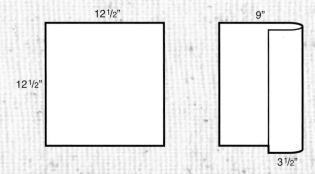

12½"

12½"

9"

3½"

Arrange the appliquéd pillow square right side up and the pressed back pieces right side down, having the pressed edges overlap in the center and lining up raw edges along all sides.

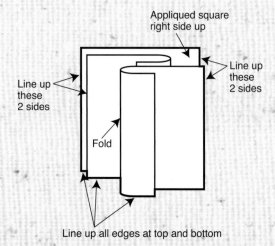

Appliqued square right side up

Line up these 2 sides

Line up these 2 sides

Fold

Line up all edges at top and bottom

Pin in place and stitch with a ¼" seam all around the pillow. Trim the corners. Turn right side out through the opening. Insert a 12" square pillow form.

What You Need

- 10" square of black wool
- Scraps of wool in the following colors: pumpkin, brown, yellow, rust, dark green
- Embroidery floss to match all wool
- ½ yard green ticking fabric
- 12" square pillow insert

Home Sweet Home
Framed Picture

Finished size: 14 ¼" x 18 ½" (inside frame measurement)

Please read through all directions before beginning. The supply list follows.

Templates are on page 79.

Cut a piece of tea-dyed osnaburg 18" x 22". Zigzag edges to prevent fraying.

Cut out five houses from different fabrics, following directions on page 12 for freezer paper fabric appliqué.

Sew the five houses together at the sides, stopping ¼" before the roof angles.

Use the freezer paper method to cut out two chimneys.

Pin houses and chimneys in place on osnaburg. Appliqué chimneys, turning tops and edges under ¼". Appliqué around the outside edge of the entire house strip, turning edges under ¼".

With a washable marker, trace words onto the osnaburg below the houses. Backstitch with two strands of black floss. Make cross stitches with two strands of dark red floss.

For tree trunks, cut one 3/4" x 4" strip from dark brown fabric. Cut in half cross-wise, making two 2" long trunks. Pin in place at each end of the house strip. Use the freezer paper method to cut six tree branches from green fabric, adding ¼" around the template. Pin three branches in place over each trunk, overlapping tops. Appliqué the trees, turning edges under ¼".

Use the freezer paper method to cut out the star. Pin and appliqué in place.

Use the freezer paper method to cut five doors, five large windows, and five small windows. Pin in place. Appliqué the tops and bottoms of the large windows and around all the sides of doors and small windows.

For each pair of shutters, cut a 3/4" x 6 ½" strip from the same fabric as the door. Cut in half crosswise to make two shutters 3/4" x 3 ¼" and pin them to the sides of the large window. Appliqué in place, turning edges under ¼".

For window boxes, cut a 3/4" x 1 ½" strip from the same fabric as the door and shutters. Pin and appliqué in place.

Add the following embellishments:

- All door knobs are six strand French knots made with tan floss.

- Lines on all small and large windows are straight stitched with six strands of floss in color to match the door and shutters.

- For House 1 (from left), the geraniums in the window box are six strand French knots (three for each flower) made with red floss. Stems are straight stitched with two strands of green floss.

- For House 2, flowers in the window box at the small window are made with two strands of green floss, stem-stitched for vines and straight stitched for leaves. Flowers are two-strand French knots made with rose and light blue floss. The cat in the large window is cut from black felt using the freezer paper method and whipstitched into place with one strand of black floss. Features on the face are made with two strands of tan floss (French knots for eyes, straight stitches for nose/mouth and whiskers).

For House 3, topiary circles are six strand French knots, clustered in a circle, made with green floss. Stems are straight stitched with two strands of dark brown floss. Pots are cut from dark brown felt using freezer paper method and whipstitched in place with two strands of dark brown floss.

For House 4, the wreath on the door is made by backstitching the circle with two strands of green floss and straight-stitching leaves with two strands of green floss. The bow is two lazy daisy stitches on top, two straight stitches below, and a French knot in the middle, made with six strands of dark red floss. The flowers in the window box at the small window are made with two strands of gold floss, lazy daisy stitched for petals (five for each flower). Centers are two strand French knots made with dark brown floss. Stems are straight stitched with two strands of green floss. The crow on the chimney is cut from black felt using the freezer paper method and whipstitched into place with one strand of black floss. The crow's eye is a two strand French knot made with tan floss and the legs are straight stitched with two strands of black floss.

For House 5, daisies below the window are made with two strands of ecru floss, lazy daisy stitched for petals (five for each flower). Centers are two strand French knots made with gold floss. Stems are straight stitched with two strands of green floss.

Center the fabric on a backing board to fit a 14 ¼" x 18 ½" frame. Pull the excess fabric to the back and glue or tape in place. Insert the picture into the frame.

What You Need

- 18" x 22" piece of tea-dyed osnaburg *(See mini-tutorial on page 70.)*
- Scraps of fabric for houses
- Scraps of dark brown, and green fabric for trees and gold for star
- Scraps of wool felt: black, dark brown
- Embroidery floss: tan, ecru, dark red, green, rose, light blue, black, dark brown, gold
- 14 ¼" x 18 ½" frame and board
- Glue or tape
- Washable marker
- Freezer paper
- Pins

Around the Block Tablerunner

Finished size: 16" x 40"

Please read through all instructions before beginning. Unless otherwise indicated, all seams are ¼" and fabrics are sewn right sides together.

Houses

(Make 16.)

For instructions on making the houses, see page 30 under Block 7 of the Welcome Home Sampler Quilt.

For each:

- From window fabric, cut 1 ¼" x 1 ½" rectangle.

  1 ¼" □ 1 ½"

- From house fabric, cut:
  - 1 ¼" x 1 ½" rectangle
  - 1 ½" square

  1 ¼" 1 ½"
  ■ ■ 1 ½"

- Sew these pieces to the window piece like this:

  1 ¼" 1 ¼" 1 ½"
  ■ □ ■ 1 ½"

From door fabric, cut 1 ¼" x 3 ½" rectangle.

  1 ¼"
  ▮ 3 ½"

From house fabric, cut

- one 2 ½" x 3" rectangle. Sew to the bottom of the window piece

- one 1 ¼" x 3 ½" rectangle. Sew lengthwise to the door piece

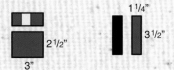

- Sew the window piece to the left side of the door piece.

From house fabric, cut 1 ½" x 4 ½" rectangle.

- Sew to the top of the window/door piece.

From roof fabric, cut 2 ½" x 4 ½" rectangle.

From tea-dyed muslin cut 2 ½" squares.

Make one Flying Geese unit for the roof of each house. *For instructions on making Flying Geese units, see page 11.*

- Sew the roof to the top of the house.

68

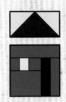

- Repeat to make 16 houses.
- Sew together side by side to make two strips of seven houses each and two remaining houses. Set aside.

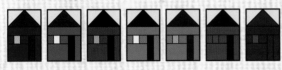

Nine-Patch Corner Blocks

(Make 4.)

For each:

- From Fabric A cut: five 2 ½" squares
- From Fabric B cut: four 2 ½" squares

See instructions on page 11.

- Repeat to make four Nine-Patch squares.

Put it Together

From tea-dyed muslin cut 4 ½" x 28 ½" rectangle

- Sew strips of seven houses to the long edges of this rectangle, roofs pointing towards the center.

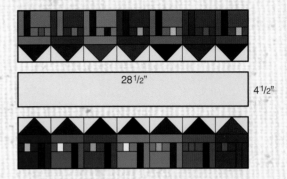

28 ½"

4 ½"

- Sew one Nine-Patch block to each side of the remaining two houses.

- Sew these strips to the short ends of the rectangle, roofs pointing towards the center.

Finish the Table Runner

See mini tutorial on page 45.

You Need

- ¼ yard muslin
- 1 ⅓ yards backing fabric
- ⅓ yard binding fabric
- 24" x 48" batting
- Lots of scraps

Mini Tutorial

Tea-dying Fabric

Place 2-3 teabags in a bowl. Pour in enough boiling water to completely cover the fabric to be dyed. Let it steep a few minutes. Crumple the fabric and stir into the tea. When the fabric is the color you want, remove from the tea. (It will lighten a bit as it dries.) Rinse under cold water until clear. Wring out and let dry. Iron.

Block 1

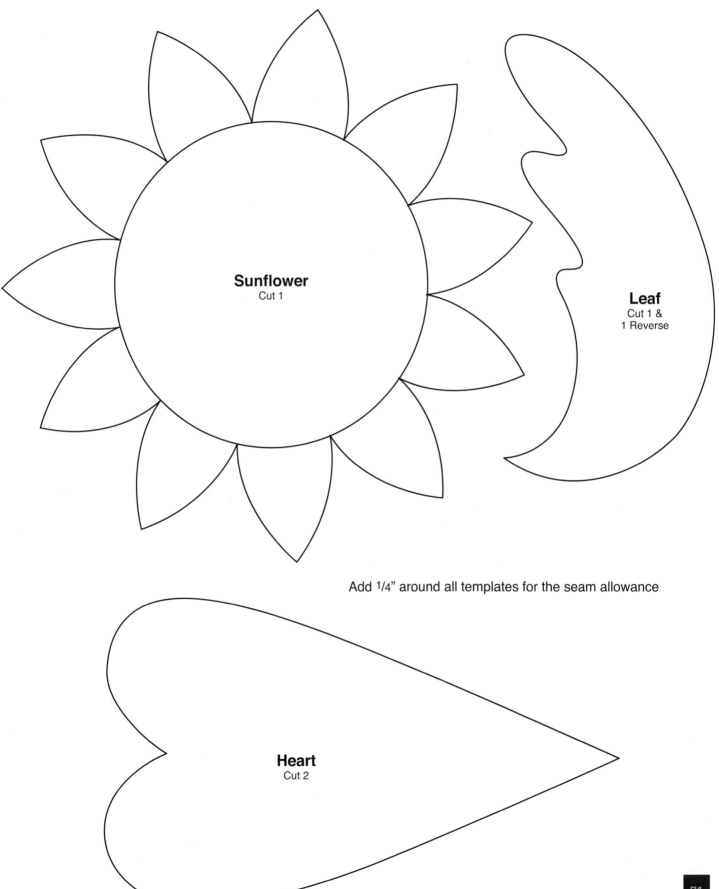

Sunflower
Cut 1

Leaf
Cut 1 &
1 Reverse

Add 1/4" around all templates for the seam allowance

Heart
Cut 2

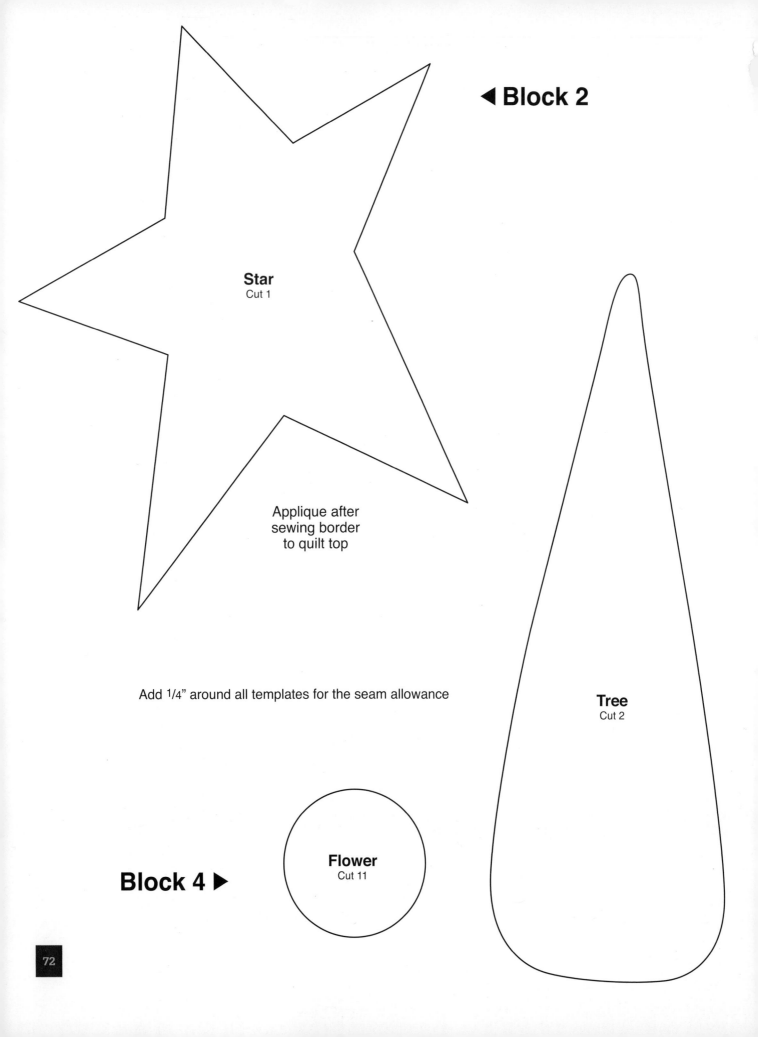

◀ **Block 2**

Star
Cut 1

Applique after
sewing border
to quilt top

Add ¼" around all templates for the seam allowance

Tree
Cut 2

Block 4 ▶

Flower
Cut 11